BUILD HIM *Up*

31 DAYS OF BLESSING YOUR HUSBAND

TABATHA HULL

To my husband, Derek. Thank you for your servant's heart. You humble me and it is a genuine joy to live life by your side.

Table of Contents

Preface

What was it like the moment you first realized that you were in love with your spouse?

Do you remember the joys that surrounded this special time? The smile that slowly slid across your face at the mention of his name? How your heart skipped a beat as he drew near?

I distinctly remember the very day that I realized I was in love with the man who had become my best friend. Surprisingly, it wasn't when he sent me flowers... came to my rescue... or surprised me with a kind gesture. Those are all sweet memories, but the moment I knew I was in love for the first time was when...

I couldn't stop thinking of ways to serve him.

I desired to make him happy and delighted to go out of my way to do so. Life ceased to be about me.

I wish I could say that every day since that moment more than 11 years ago has been filled with pure joy and bliss, but we all know that's not reality. Life gets busy. Children enter the picture. Our time becomes divided. Priorities change.

Marriage takes work. And if we aren't intentional in pursuing this relationship, it will most likely begin to deteriorate over time.

It's not all that common in our current culture to admit our flaws, but the truth is that I am a sinner. I have weaknesses and will fail my husband. And you know what? I also married a sinner. Although the depth of our love for each other is truly beautiful, we can never perfectly meet the needs of one another. And truthfully it is unfair to put expectations on our spouse that they aren't capable of meeting.

The only Person who can ever fully satisfy all of our longings is the Man who died to be our Savior.

My goal in writing is to remind all of us that we are each in desperate need of redemption. We are living in a broken world that seems to get darker by the minute. And yet, in the midst of the chaos, God in His goodness chose to give us a best friend to do life with.

I'd like to encourage you to approach this book a bit differently than most. This book isn't guaranteed to transform your marriage. But I am praying that it will leave an impression on your heart. I pray that as wives we will understand the beauty and blessings of the role we've been given. I pray that we would seek God as to how to best love our husbands and give them the respect and affirmation they crave.

Marriage is a precious gift. May we do all that we can to glorify the Giver and build up our men.

How To Use This Book

For the next month I'd like to encourage you to intentionally pursue your spouse and meet his needs in a fresh way. This will take preparation, time, patience, and love invested into it.

Please take a look at the table of contents and try to map out your plans for the next month. Scheduling all 31 days in advance would be ideal, but it's not entirely realistic. Life happens, so I'd suggest shooting for a week at a time or at the very least try to plan 3-4 days out. You may need to flip through certain chapters to get a clearer understanding of each day. (The first paragraph or two of each chapter will explain in detail what you are to do).

I ask you to do this step so that you are more inclined to follow through the entire month and not get too far off track or give up altogether. It is completely okay to modify the ideas or do them out of order if necessary. And if you miss a day don't fret! Just get back up and continue on your mission.

I realize that the idea of 31 days may seem overwhelming to some, but I promise it is very doable! Exactly half of these ideas require no planning whatsoever. Friend, if it takes you three months to make it through this book that is okay! The goal is simply to finish and have a teachable heart along the way.

Each day you will be given a new way to show love to your husband. Some of these may require additional time invested into them, while others will take minimal effort. And there may even be a couple that you're already doing! The idea is to complete the entire 31 days without your husband having any clue as to what you're up to!

There will also be a daily Bible verse and prayer prompts as to how you can be praying for him each day. Obviously each of our husbands and marriages have different needs. I encourage you to be mindful of both the struggles and strengths of yours and intentionally set aside time each day to pray for those needs. The prompts are just ideas if you're looking for some specific ways to be in prayer each day.

Ladies, this is going to take some energy, creativity, and planning, but it will be more than worth it in the end. I am praying that by the end of the 31 day challenge your love and appreciation for your husband will be strengthened.

We were created to serve one another. No marriage is perfect, but when two people look at this sweet union through the lens of loving and serving, it is truly beautiful beyond words.

And please know that even if your husband does not respond well to your acts of service, you have undoubtedly pleased and honored your Creator by faithfully loving your spouse. Make no doubt that God can still use your efforts and obedience for your good and His glory.

Day 1

Love Letter

Let's begin our challenge by writing a good old fashioned love letter. Although the art of handwritten letters may have gone out of style for pure convenience sake, their effect remains the same. There will always be something special about receiving a letter in the handwriting of those you love. Especially when those words are from your spouse and best friend.

A handwritten letter will likely catch your husband off guard and cause him to pause his busy day to enjoy reading it. Take some time to think about what exactly it is you'd like to say. Make it meaningful and make certain that you're, in some way, communicating the love you hold for him. Then place it somewhere that he is sure to find without handing it to him directly.

I believe that we often unintentionally downplay the importance of our words. Our words have the power to build up, but just as easily tear down. As wives we can be guilty of tearing down our husbands without even realizing it. The pressures of life have a way of clouding our view of what's truly important. Before we realize it we begin to take our marriages for granted with a little less filtering of the tongue than we had in the beginning.

I have seen this ring true in my own marriage more times than I'd like to admit. During our months of dating and into our newlywed years I was so careful not to speak words that may hurt my husband. After our children came along, however, and many sleepless nights along with them, I have said things in frustration, irritability, or anger that I have later regretted.

Let's be gentle and thoughtful with our words. We cannot undo them.

Genuinely seek to begin encouraging your spouse more-specifically through your words. This may mean simply holding your tongue at times, or looking for an opportunity to compliment your husband on a decision he's made. You know his strengths as well as those areas that could use some improvement better than anyone else. Be his number one encourager and supporter. And please don't just assume he already knows this. We've got to verbally speak life into our husbands, ladies! On repeat.

"Let no corrupting talk come out of your mouths, but only such as is good for building up, as fits the occasion, that it may give grace to those who hear." (Ephesians 4:29)

Prayer Prompts:

- To more clearly see opportunities to encourage your husband
- To be able to better filter your thoughts and hold your tongue
- For your love for your spouse to be strengthened
- To honor God with the words you speak to others
- For wisdom and patience as you begin this next month of serving your husband

Day 2

Treat and a Movie

What is your husband's absolute favorite dessert or special treat? Something that he doesn't have the opportunity to enjoy too frequently, but always brings a smile to his face? Ice cream from a local shop? Mouthwatering cake from a favorite restaurant or bakery? Whatever it is, make sure to pick it up and surprise him tonight! It will be the perfect addition for movie night. Rent his favorite movie and cuddle up for a relaxing evening.

It is often the smallest things that can make the biggest impact. A sweet and thoughtful gesture can make a world of difference for the one on the receiving end.

I'll never forget a few years back my husband coming home a bit late from work one evening. At the time his job was quite taxing, so I just assumed that it must have been a rough day. To my surprise he walked in the door and handed me my favorite ice cream on the planet! (Frozen custard to be exact, *ohhhh YUM!*) It was divine... and also not available in the dead of winter when he brought it home to me. You see, the frozen custard shop a few miles down the road from us closes for the winter months every year. I wasn't expecting my next taste of swirled chocolate and peanut butter cup goodness for at least another two months! I'm pretty certain that my eyes grew wide as saucers and my jaw dropped when he handed it to me.

So how exactly did he do it you might be wondering? Well... I quickly found out that he searched around and discovered there was another location several miles north of his new job. He left work in a hurry, driving in the opposite direction of home, so that he could surprise me that night. And here's the sweetest part of all- he drove over 35 minutes home with the HEAT OFF in the freezing cold weather just so that it wouldn't melt! My heart thoroughly melted instead.

My husband certainly didn't think he was doing any grand gesture that evening, but his thoughtfulness told my heart a different story. His simple decision to lay aside his own conveniences in order to show love in some small way made a huge impact in my little world.

Obviously not everyone becomes giddy with excitement over ice cream, but I am certain that there is something just as simple that can bring a little joy to your husband. If movies aren't really his thing, you could try heading outside after dark for some stargazing.

Tailor it to his likes and interests and make it special. *Make him smile.*

"But the fruit of the Spirit is love, joy, peace, patience, kindness, goodness, faithfulness, gentleness, self-control; against such things there is no law." Galatians 5:22-23

Prayer Prompts:

- For you and your husband to have genuine joy in life that isn't based upon your changing circumstances
- Thank God for giving you a best friend to do life with
- To have a servant's heart

Day 3

"Thank You"

There are two little words that have more power together than we often give them credit for. A simple "thank you" can go a long way in a marriage. Today your goal is to take some time to either call or text your husband for the sole purpose of letting him know how grateful you are for him.

Share at least one specific reason that you appreciate him. Your conversation doesn't need to be super lengthy, but make sure he knows that you take notice of the things he does for your family and around your home.

In the busyness of life we sometimes neglect to show our appreciation like we once did. It's easy to assume our spouse already knows all of these things, but the truth is that maybe he doesn't. We may have the best of intentions. We may *think* about how much we appreciate him, but unfortunately good intentions don't always mean much if they aren't backed up with accompanying words and actions.

Whether it's a short and sweet "Honey, thank you for mowing the grass each week" or "thank you for the way that you love and lead our family and pour into our children"- your husband needs to hear those words of affirmation and appreciation.

You've most likely heard of the five love languages (Words of affirmation, Quality time, Physical touch, Acts of service, Receiving gifts). If you haven't I'd encourage you to do some research to get a better grasp on the topic. It is extremely helpful!

Dr. Gary Chapman crafted the concept in his book *The Five Love Languages* [1] where he goes on to explain how each of us has a primary way that we receive love. This often, by default, also means that we show love to others in the same way.

Now, obviously any way that we show love to others is a good thing, BUT continually neglecting to show them love *in the very way that they crave* can leave our loved ones with a half empty "love tank". Our husband needs more than just the status quo in the love department. It's our job and privilege as his wife to make sure that his needs are being met and his tank is filled to the brim. Or better yet, overflowing.

Your husband's love language may just happen to be "words of affirmation". If so, keep in mind that he needs to hear these words even more frequently to feel loved and appreciated. However, even if this isn't the main way that he receives love, he still needs to hear those reassuring words of praise and gratitude from time to time. *We all do.*

The idea behind this entire challenge is that by slowing down to really focus on our spouse and our marriage we will realize what a blessing we've been given. Loving, serving, and placing another's needs before our own can't help but bring about gratitude.

"You are my God, and I will give thanks to you; you are my God; I will extol you. Oh give thanks to the LORD, for he is good-for his steadfast love endures forever!" Psalm 118:28-29

Prayer Prompts:

- While you are thanking your husband today, also take time to *thank God for your husband*
- For wisdom to understand the primary way that your spouse receives love
- For a humble heart to meet your husband's needs with grace

Day 4

Housework

Housework is one of those monotonous necessities when it comes to running a household. Nobody really enjoys it, but it's a wonderful reminder of the blessings of having a family and owning a home. Although some couples take turns doing whatever work needs done around the home at any given moment, the majority of us eventually fall into some kind of repetitive pattern... he does this and she does that.

Today your job is to take over some of your husband's housework. It could be as simple as taking out the trash, washing his car, or may involve a little bit of sweat equity if you decide to engage in some yard work. If he is typically the chef of the family, try your hand at a new recipe!

You most likely already know what would be the biggest help to him. *Whatever it is put some effort into it, have a sweet spirit about it, and do your work cheerfully.* He will take notice.

He usually beats me to it, but I try to take our trash out to the curb on pick up mornings. It's the most simple gesture, but for some reason always brings a smile to my husband's face once he realizes that it's already done and is one less thing on his plate for the day. So often it's not even the actual act itself that makes all the difference, but the simple thought behind it.

Think of your husband today and a simple act of kindness to make him smile. Seeing you do housework that he often handles will show him that you do appreciate the work that he does as well as the time he puts into taking care of these things around your home.

For any of you who may be in a difficult phase and feel as if your spouse wouldn't take notice of or truly appreciate your efforts, I'd encourage you to still do it. Do it for your Creator.

"So, whether you eat or drink, or whatever you do, do all to the glory of God." 1 Corinthians 10:31

Prayer Prompts:

- To have a grateful attitude as you do housework
- To view the mundane tasks in life as blessings (washing dishes means that God has provided food for your family to eat etc.)
- To do all of your work throughout the day to the best of your ability for God's glory

Day 5

Something You Admire

Compliments come naturally during the "falling in love" stage of a relationship. They do not come as easily during the sleep deprived, stress induced, "what was he thinking?!" phase that comes later down the road. Today I'd like to encourage you to take a few minutes to remember what exactly it is that you admire about your husband. Then, when the time is right, tell him!

Is it a certain character trait? His friendly nature? Work ethic? Fatherly instincts? What initially drew you to him? What is it about him that still stops you in your tracks as gratitude begins swelling up inside of you?

I think by now you're beginning to realize that most of these challenges don't take a whole lot of effort. Many of them are likely even things that you once did on a fairly regular basis.

There's an analogy that I read in a book back in high school that has stuck with me all these years.

It's one that I repeatedly remind my children of when they're struggling in a particular area, and one that convicts my own heart when I am struggling too.

It's called the "teabag analogy" and goes a little something like this: Imagine that your heart is like a teabag. The piping hot water that is poured into the tea cup represents the trials of life. The water itself plays only a small role in the whole process of making tea- it merely draws out of the bag *what is already there*. In the same way the pressures of life simply squeeze out of our own hearts what is already there. Those pressures don't create anything in and of themselves. When our hearts are full of bitterness, frustration, and pride that's exactly what's going to come out when those pressures are closing in around us.

I have learned throughout my years of being a wife and mother that life becomes more challenging because the pressures around us increase. When we choose to focus on the inconveniences and difficulties life throws our way we're also unintentionally focusing on ourselves. When our eyes are on self we very rarely have the ability to clearly see the needs of those around us (including our spouse), and the downward spiral begins.

But here's the incredible thing- in the midst of those trials we don't have to succumb to our natural sinful ways of handling things. If we're faithful to stay close to our Savior, He can give us a sweet grace and peace in the midst of all the chaos. He can replace the anger with forgiveness. Feelings of despair with hope and contentment. And exhaustion with comfort and rest.

He can help reset our focus to better remember the blessings of our marriage as well as those little (and big) things we admire and appreciate about our spouse.

It's not a matter of "if" but "when". When the trials of life hit you hard what will come out of your heart?

"Keep your heart with all vigilance, for from it flow the springs of life." Proverbs 4:23

Prayer Prompts:

- To handle the trials of life through God's strength and not your own
- To learn to rest in God's faithfulness and goodness when situations are out of your control
- For peace and comfort in the midst of hardships
- For a desire to keep loving and serving your spouse even while going through these trials

Day 6

Pray

You've likely been praying for your husband each day throughout this past week, and I encourage you to continue doing so. Today, however, we're going to do something a bit different. Ask your husband if there is anything specific that you can be in prayer for and then ask if you can pray out loud *for him*.

Hearing the prayers of others on our behalf is a pretty humbling experience. Take this opportunity to show your spouse how much you love and appreciate him as you humbly approach the God of the universe on his behalf. Thank God for allowing you the privilege of having a best friend by your side to "do life" with. Pray for specific areas that you know would be an encouragement to him, and then rest in knowing that God hears the prayers of those who belong to Him (I Peter 3:12). And He is faithful.

I'd like to pause here for a moment to say that we're living in a day and age where our hearts and minds are a constant battleground.

Our enemy wants nothing more than to destroy our marriages and families. He delights to keep us busy and distracted. He deceives us into thinking that we've got it all under control. *It is in these unsuspecting moments that we give him a foot into the door of our hearts.*

It is imperative that we are faithful to continually pray for our spouse. We can pray for our husband's overall character and for his faith to be continually strengthened.

We can pray that he will...

- Take his thoughts captive- We are constantly bombarded with images and voices trying to lead us astray each day. This is especially true for our visually stimulated husbands. Let's pray for our husband to be prepared when the temptations arise and push away the unhealthy thoughts through God's strength and the truths of His Word.

- Guard his heart- If there's one thing I've learned in marriage, it's that men don't share as much as women do. However, the stresses of life affect them just the same. Unlike women, men will often try to conceal their exhaustion, fear, and worry. We can pray the he will guard his heart and not allow the hardships to result in anger, frustration, or pulling away.

- Be convicted of sin- Yes, God gave us a conscience to know right from wrong. BUT we can easily sear it when it goes against the desires of our sinful flesh. We can pray for our spouse to have a tender conscience towards sin and the heart to repent. That he will desire to restore a right relationship with his Savior.

- Desire Humility- If you really think about it almost every type of sin we commit can be rooted in some form of pride. As much as I hate to admit it I still struggle with this too. Pride is foolishly believing that I can handle things on my own. Pride is the way I can somehow see the spec in someone else's eye while neglecting the log in my own. Pride is making assumptions about others when I don't know the full story. I think it's safe to say that in their desire to provide for and lead their families men struggle with pride too, many times to an even greater extent. We can pray for our husband to humbly submit to God's leading and recognize His gifts and goodness. We can pray that he will put God first and then place others above himself.

- Be faithful in his daily walk with God- It takes intentional effort to stay focused in this area. So many noises and distractions will attempt to drown out the importance of faithfully studying God's Word and spending time in prayer. Pray that your husband will be refreshed and strengthened as he pursues His Creator. That God will create within him the desire to be a man after His own heart.

- Have wisdom in leading his family- As women we seem to struggle with the desire to be in control of situations. And we just so happen to have some powerful emotions. Although these emotions *can* be healthy, they are never meant to lead us. Our husbands, on the other hand, were gifted with the ability to make calculated decisions a bit easier, which comes in handy in their God given responsibility to lead our families. We can pray for them to seek God's guidance when making these decisions instead of relying on their own inclinations or preferences.

- Be a diligent worker- This isn't always one that we think upon too often, but we're told several times in Scripture how God desires us to be diligent workers in the tasks that He's called us to. We can pray that our husband will honor God in his work by performing both the trivial or important jobs with joy and gratitude.

- Develop godly friendships- We know that peers and companions have an enormous impact on our children's character. Well, not all that much changes as we grow into adulthood. Those we spend the most time with and seek advice from still have a tremendous impact on us whether we realize it or not. We can pray for our husband to develop godly friendships with men that have a genuine desire to encourage each other and point one another to Christ.

- Find joy in his wife- Ladies, this one is for us! We can also pray that we will graciously do our part in meeting our husband's needs, encouraging him, respecting him, and loving him the way he needs to be loved.

"Continue steadfastly in prayer, being watchful in it with thanksgiving." Colossians 4:2

Prayer prompts:

- For your husband to guard his heart and take his thoughts captive

Day 7

Hobby Date

We all have our favorite past times and hobbies. Today spend some time doing one of your husband's favorite hobbies with him. Whether it's big or small, just focus on truly enjoying your time spent together while doing something that is sure to put a smile on his face.

If he's a golfer, take him to the driving range to hit a bucket of balls together. If he enjoys woodworking, ask if you can assist him with a project he's working on. Go for a hike, join him on a fishing trip, or go to a sporting event. If he works long hours and likes to unwind by watching a ball game or favorite TV show that you typically prefer to sit out, try sitting *in* this time. You know his favorites. Just remove yourself and your preferences from the equation for the day and make it about him.

As wives we have a tendency to take over many aspects of our marriage relationship if we're not careful.

"Where should we go out for dinner?" "What color should we paint the living room walls?" "What should we do with that bonus check?" "What kind of discipline does our child deserve in this situation?" You better believe that we have some pretty strong opinions on all of the above scenarios and much more. Ever heard the phrase "Happy wife. Happy life."? ... I don't exactly think it was meant to be a compliment.

We touched on this a bit in our last chapter but I believe it's important to dive into this topic a little deeper. Women naturally gravitate towards being in charge and making the decisions, sometimes without ever acknowledging our husband's desires. Although we may not catch it upon first glance Genesis 3:16 echoes this struggle.

It's not a popular viewpoint, but God's perfect design is for a husband and wife to be working *together* for the greater good, not selfishly seeking to please ourselves. To take this one step further, His design is actually for the *husband* to be the one to lead the family (1 Corinthians 11:3). Not us. Many women look down upon this opinion as if it's an insult to us wives. This couldn't be further from the truth. Ladies, we are emotional creatures. Our men, on the other hand, have a natural logical drive that enables them to make decisions, overall, a little bit easier than us.

Although we are in this together and my husband always asks for my input on things, just knowing that he has the final say and will take care of our family honestly takes a load off of my shoulders. One less thing I have to worry about and one more reason for me to admire his leadership and love for our family.

God's design for men to lead their families in no way diminishes our worth or the importance of our role as wives. On the contrary, our roles beautifully complement one another and allow us to use our God given gifts to the fullest.

Make today about him. And make sure he knows that you truly value his input, opinions, and leadership abilities.

"Love is patient and kind; love does not envy or boast; it is not arrogant or rude. It does not insist on its own way; it is not irritable or resentful, it does not rejoice at wrongdoing, but rejoices with the truth. Love bears all things, believes all things, hopes all things, endures all things. Love never ends." 1 Corinthians 13:4-8

Prayer Prompts:

- To love your husband with a Christ-like love
- To find joy in placing him first
- For God to change your desires when you're tempted to insist on your own way
- To have a grateful heart for your God given role

Day 8

Initiate

You've made it a full week into our challenge! Thank you for your desire to faithfully pour into your spouse and marriage. From this moment forward I'd like to encourage you to focus on initiating intimacy from time to time. This is one that doesn't come naturally for the majority of us wives, yet this simple act can have a huge impact on our men. And for the record, I sincerely doubt that there will ever be such a thing as initiating too often in your husband's mind!

It's no surprise that the world around us has marred God's beautiful design of intimacy, while at the same time portraying men in an unfair light. Yes, it is true that men typically desire physical intimacy more so than women, but it is equally true that they are made this way. Our brains are wired differently. And when our Creator chose to make us with those unique differences He didn't make a mistake.

(On a side note, please know that in no way am I condoning the thoughts and actions of those who are clearly overstepping God's boundaries and design for intimacy.

The sad reality is that many men, and even women, are in direct sin when it comes to God's design for sexuality.)

Ladies, I get it. I know that you are tired! However, if we have enough energy to read a book, work on a project, or scroll through social media for 20 minutes after putting the kids to bed, I'm sure that we can muster up enough energy to be with him. Putting his needs before our own actually has a way of causing us to stop and realize just how much we appreciate this man that God has so graciously given us to enjoy life with.

Isn't it amazing how selflessly meeting the needs of another can increase the depth of our admiration and love for them? We are living in a culture that tries to lure a man's thoughts and heart away from his spouse every place they turn. Let's make sure that we are lovingly filling up this "love tank" as well.

May we be available, generous, and kind. May our husband delight to find satisfaction within our arms instead of falling into the temptation to go search for it elsewhere.

"Therefore a man shall leave his father and his mother and hold fast to his wife, and they shall become one flesh." Genesis 2:24

Prayer Prompts:

- For the energy and desire to be intimate
- To have a right heart attitude about meeting your husbands needs
- For an understanding heart regarding how we were created differently in this area

Day 9

Make A Video

We make a lot of assumptions in life. Some are healthy and safe, while others miss the mark entirely. We often assume that our loved ones know just how much we love them, but this isn't always the case. Whether it's through kind words or acts of service we've got to be intentional in communicating our love and appreciation for our spouse. Today, you have a small project to work on. In an effort to express your love and gratitude to your husband you'll need to create a cell phone video of you (and your children if you choose) sharing what you love most about him.

Please be sure to make it personal and mention certain qualities, skills, personality traits, or special memories. Find a comfy chair with good lighting and prop your phone up in front of you to capture your message. You may choose to send it to him while you're apart for the day, or tell him you made him a little something and share it with him when he comes home. You'd be surprised at how a few minutes of effort can brighten his day.

For the past 10 years of marriage I've created a similar video for my husband's birthday. But instead of verbally sharing what I love most about him, I put together slideshows of our favorite memories over the past year and set them to music- a favorite or meaningful song. And then there was this one year when the tables turned and my husband surprised *me* with a video for *my* birthday before he left for a week long work trip.

My heart about burst at his thoughtfulness as he sat me down and the video began. His kind words immediately brought a smile to my face, and then as his video faded... (que the tears)... another video appeared with the sweet faces of my children sharing what they "love most about Mommy". If that wasn't enough, (tears streaming now) ten more videos transitioned as my family and friends also shared some kind words for me on my birthday. To this day that was the best birthday gift I have ever received. My husband told me he just wanted me to feel loved and appreciated. And boy did he nail it!

Our words and actions can have a powerful impact on others. Please have fun creating your video and use your words to build up your man.

"Therefore encourage one another and build one another up, just as you are doing." 1 Thessalonians 5:11

Prayer Prompts:

- To better see little opportunities to encourage your husband
- To stop making assumptions in life

- To clearly communicate your appreciation for you husband on a regular basis

Day 10

A Night Off

We all have different night time routines and responsibilities. Your task today is to simply do your best to give your husband a night off from his.

If he typically cleans up the kitchen after dinner, offer to clean it up instead. If he needs to mow the grass, take a turn. If he bathes the children or tucks them in at night, grab the PJs. And if he works late into the evening ... maybe you could convince him to lay it all aside for tonight (wink wink). I think you get the idea.

I'm aware that sometimes a spouse may be less than motivated to get much done after a long day at work. If your thoughts are convincing you that there aren't any responsibilities to relieve your husband from (because he likes to take it easy) I'd encourage you to get creative and take care of something that would be a help to him. (And to not allow that bitterness to creep in.)

Being on the receiving end of an act of service can't help but trigger something inside of our hearts. Sometimes it's gratitude. Joy. Humility. Love.... And sometimes it's *conviction* because we know we don't deserve that kind of generosity. So whatever the case may be with your husband please know that you can't go wrong by serving. God can always use it for good.

By now you've likely realized that a common thread woven throughout this book is the idea of serving our spouse. This idea may be counter cultural, but that doesn't mean it's faulty. The One who *created* the human heart gets to determine what *satisfies* the human heart. Placing ourselves first will never bring about lasting satisfaction and joy.

Please trust your Creator and look for ways to begin serving your husband more. Obviously, there is a whole lot of joy that results from being on the receiving end of someone else's kindness, but we also get to experience a whole lot of joy when we're on the *giving* end as well.

"It is more blessed to give than to receive." Acts 20:35

Prayer Prompts:

- To have a heart that desires to serve
- To see with fresh eyes that life, as well as marriage, isn't about gratifying ourselves

Day 11

Steal Him Away

It's no surprise that us ladies like to be pursued. How many classic fairy tales, books, and movies involve a lovely fair maiden and her dashing prince charming wooing, pursuing, and coming to her rescue? There is something ingrained within us to desire the chase and affections of a man.

I'd even dare to say that men enjoy the *pursuing* as much as we enjoy the pursuit, and they certainly get excited when it involves physical touch of any kind! Today you get to be the one doing the pursuing. When he is least expecting it, grab your husband's hand and steal him away for a kiss. Whether it is sweet and tender or full of passion you're likely to leave him all smiles in the process.

My husband began working from home nearly two years ago... and I'm a homeschool mom. Needless to say we see quite a bit of each other. I take absolutely zero credit for this and give all the glory to God, but thankfully even after all this time together we never tire of each other.

He is still my best friend and it brings me great comfort to know that he is near. (I may or may not lead him to the laundry room on occasion to sneak in a kiss when he comes down from the office for a bite to eat.) The look on his face shows his approval and appreciation!

Ladies, when it comes down to it our husbands are pretty easy to please. *They desire our praise and our affections.* Your husband wants to know that you are proud to be his wife, that you still find satisfaction in his arms, and that if you had to do it all over you would choose him again and again.

Prior to marriage most people associate *physical touch* with *physical intimacy.* The idea of becoming "one flesh" (Genesis 2:24) is a foreign concept to us until we allow ourselves to become intimate in every sense of the word as we step into marriage. Becoming one with your husband is your entire being welding together with his- yes physically, but equally on an emotional, spiritual, and intellectual level- he gets all of you. And you get all of him.

I say all of that to remind you that a simple unexpected kiss can speak a thousand words to your husband. Be intentional in showing him affection.

"Then the Lord God said, "It is not good that the man should be alone; I will make him a helper fit for him." Genesis 2:18

Prayer Prompts:

- To more clearly see opportunities to show affection

- To remember those initial "pursuing" days in the beginning of your relationship and seek to find that kind of fulfillment in each other once again.

Day 12

Light Some Candles

There's something special about the flickering glow of candles, their lovely scent, and a back massage. Tonight light some candles and invite your husband into the bedroom for a massage.

Have you ever wondered what exactly it is that begins to drive a wedge between a couple? I believe it's quite simply nothing more than a shift in our priorities. During our time of dating on into our early months of marriage we intentionally pour into one another. We make time for our husband. He makes time for us. We do things for one another and delight to be together. Eventually, for whatever reason, we stop trying so hard. Slowly we begin to drift apart.

But what if there wasn't a newlywed phase? I guess I'm asking you to look at it this way... A phase is a period of time that has an end date. What if our marriage was so full of purpose and joy that we lived our entire lives together like we did in the very beginning of our relationship? What if that special "phase" never ended?

Friend, I realize that none of my thoughts in this book are rocket science. These are all simple reminders to try to nudge us back in line with God's original design for marriage. A design that is truly beautiful and meant for our good and His glory. Just like that candle you light tonight to illuminate the darkness and offer a soothing environment, in a world of such despair God can use our marriage to be a light and point others directly to His Son if we are willing to prioritize Him above all else, and love our husbands well.

In my Bible reading I was recently struck by a simple verse squished in between a couple of paragraphs about God's grace. 1 Peter 4:8 says "Above all, keep loving one another earnestly, since love covers a multitude of sins." The word *earnestly* here is interchangeable with the word *fervently*. *Fervent* stems from the word *ektenés* in the original Greek which holds a pretty powerful connotation. *Ektenés* is a combination of the root words *ek* meaning "out from and to" (regarding the outcome of something) and *teinō* which means "to stretch" (think of our English word *tension*). When we put these two little words together the result is something like this: "(to) stretch out, i.e. fully completely taut; at maximum potential, without slack because (it's) fully extended to its necessary outcome." [1]

So what if we began applying 1 Peter 4:8 to our marriage and started loving our husband earnestly? Fervently. What if our love for him was stretched out to its maximum potential without any slack? *In spite of his flaws and sin.* And what if our obedience to do so prompted him to do the same in return? *In spite of ours.*

This single Bible verse has summed up my entire purpose in writing this book- to remind us that God's plan for us as husband and wife is to whole-heartedly love one other and place each other's needs and desires above our own. If we are faithful to do so the result is something so precious that words can't quite do it justice.

"Above all, keep loving one another earnestly, since love covers a multitude of sins." 1 Peter 4:8

Prayer Prompts:

- For a desire to wholly love your husband without conditions
- To clearly see ways that selfishness and bitterness have crept into your own heart in regards to marriage and seek forgiveness
- For your marriage to be a light that will point others to Christ

Day 13

Recreate Your First Date

This is one that will take a bit of preparation, but will be more than worth it! Take a moment to reminisce about your very first date together. Where did you go? What did you do? What were your first impressions of the man who would later become your husband? After you've had some time to think it over do your very best to recreate it and take him on a surprise date. I realize that this may not be entirely doable depending on the circumstances, but encourage you to put some effort into making it special. If your initial date isn't possible to recreate then pick another one of your first few dates and aim for that one.

I vividly remember my first date with my husband nearly 12 years ago. At the time we were living more than an hour away from each other, so we agreed to meet in the middle at a *Panera Bread* location. Upon meeting in the parking lot we complimented one another on our vehicles. (He had a pretty Mustang with one powerful engine! I was driving my dream Firebird with a Ram Air hood that I still miss to this day.) We headed inside to order.

He got a soda and I got a smoothie. We sat outside at a picnic table to chat which turned into a three hour long conversation.

I drove home that night with a smile on my face. He was kind. He seemed sweet. He made me laugh. He was handsome. And he clearly loved his family (which meant that he was potentially a family man). I was not emotionally giddy or "head over heels", but was simply grateful to have met someone who seemed genuinely kind.

Little did I know at the time that this would be the start of a beautiful friendship that eventually blossomed into my first real love a few months down the road. Looking back I am forever grateful that God so graciously guarded my heart until it was safe to be handed over to the man who would become my husband.

While we're speaking on matters of the heart I'd like to pause for a moment to turn your thoughts back to the Man who died to be your Savior. Even after we're married the majority of us still have a tendency to expect our spouse to be the one who will completely satisfy us and meet all of our needs. We become shocked, hurt, and even disillusioned when he begins to fail to meet or even acknowledge those needs. This is where we've got to realize that, as wonderful as marriage is, God's design was never for our husband to be the one to satisfy all of our deepest longings and wholly complete us. That role is reserved for our Savior.

God's design for marriage is for us to have a best friend to do life with. It is for us to encourage one another, help each other, to express and receive love.

When done right a marriage can even be a picture of the incredible love Christ holds for us (His "church"). However, even the world's most amazing spouse can never take the place of having a personal relationship with the One who willingly chose to rescue us from the bondage of our sin and offer us an eternal home in His presence. Every person who has ever walked the face of the planet was created with a void inside of them that can only ever be filled with the One who stepped down from glory to offer Himself as a sacrifice in our place.

Our pain, heartaches, loneliness, and emptiness, can only be remedied by the very One who spoke our lives into existence. May we turn to Him to meet the needs that only He can satisfy.

"Come to me, all who labor and are heavy laden, and I will give you rest. Take my yoke upon you, and learn from me, for I am gentle and lowly in heart, and you will find rest for your souls. For my yoke is easy, and my burden is light." Matthew 11:28-30

Prayer Prompts:

- To pour into your relationship like you did in the beginning
- To fully understand your roles as husband and wife as well as the role of your Savior
- To learn to ultimately seek Jesus to satisfy those deep desires and find your completion in Him

Day 14

Let Him Know

We all know that men are visual. They make no effort to hide their satisfaction in the female form. But what we don't always realize is that they *also need to feel desirable* by us. Today your task is pretty simple: let your husband know that you find him attractive. Verbally tell him, and then offer a flirtatious smile or a quick bum squeeze for good measure (just an FYI that last one always seems to be a winner). However you say it just make sure that you leave no doubt in his mind as to your attraction to him.

Going back to the love languages we touched on a few days ago, some men primarily receive love through words of affirmation. And even if this isn't your husband's primary love language you can be certain that it's still a need. He needs your approval. Not because he's insecure, but because he was made this way. We all desire the approval of those we love.

This could also serve as a reminder that our husbands need to be hearing a lot of things from us on a regular basis.

In the beginning of your relationship you likely used your words to build him up without any effort. You may have complimented him on how a certain blue shirt made his eyes pop. How his strength made you feel safe and secure. How the way he led your family gave you comfort. Or how that decision he made was a wise choice.

Those uplifting words may not come as easily as the busyness and pressures of life increase. I'd like to challenge you to go against the grain on this one and make sure that you are intentionally speaking life into your husband... on the days that he deserves it and even on the days when clearly he doesn't. Our edifying words can get through to the heart in a powerful way and go a long way in strengthening a marriage.

The Golden Rule applies to us in marriage just as much as it applied to us when we were children struggling with some sort of wrong inside of our heart. If we began to "do to our husband as we would have him do to us" (Matthew 7:12) would our marriage look different? Would the words we speak, the thoughts we allow to swirl around in our minds, or the ones we actually put into action look different?

If this is an area that you've let slide over the years (as many of us do) please make an effort to pour into your husband. If encouraging words are difficult for you because you're in a difficult phase of marriage please make it a matter of prayer. Pray for God to help change your heart and give you grace to extend to your husband. Remember the grace *you've* been shown (Ephesians 2:8).

Go back to the beginning and take some time to dwell upon the beauty of having a life partner.

"Two are better than one, because they have a good reward for their toil. For if they fall, one will lift up his fellow. But woe to him who is alone when he falls and has not another to lift him up!" Ecclesiastes 4:9-10

Prayer Prompts:

- To get in the habit once again of speaking words to our husband that will truly encourage his heart
- For grace to extend when he doesn't deserve it
- To truly grasp God's goodness in offering us grace

Day 15

Your Head On His Shoulder

I remember hearing once that men prefer shoulder-to-shoulder interaction whereas women prefer face-to-face. I can't say I fully understood this concept prior to getting married, but after several years of marriage the accuracy of this statement is now crystal clear.

For example, my idea of feeling close to my husband may look something like this: cuddling up together on the couch while looking into each other's eyes and talking about our deepest hopes and desires for our family. My husband's idea of feeling close on the other hand may look a little something like this: sitting beside one another on that same couch while watching a football game on TV. Obviously these are two very different ideas of spending time together, but they are each valid needs. Today please make an effort to see this need through your husband's eyes.

At some point in the day sit next to him and lay your head on his shoulder for no other reason than to be close. Sit side-by-side without feeling the need to have a long drawn out conversation. Just be with him.

I was recently thinking upon Proverbs 31. You know the chapter that makes us shrink back in disappointment because we feel like utter failures in comparison? Well there is a single line in that chapter that has always stood out to me. When referring to the "excellent wife" King Lamuel makes a point to say that "The heart of her husband trusts in her" (v. 11). When two people deeply trust one another words aren't always necessary. And there is often a sweet peace that follows.

As I think about the numerous times that I've been guilty of dumping all of my emotional woes onto my husband I am reminded that although he enjoys being a comfort to me, my words are not always an encouragement to his heart. I imagine that what does his heart the most good is when I silently slip my hand into his and cozy up next to him because I am completely content in our relationship and filled with gratitude. When I rest my head on his shoulder to express the amount of love I hold for him because words aren't even necessary.

Friend, does the heart of your husband trust in you? Is he completely content and at peace to simply have you next to him? If trust is an area that either of you struggle with please bring it before your Creator as you seek to repair that bridge.

"An excellent wife who can find? She is far more precious than jewels. The heart of her husband trusts in her, and he will have no lack of gain." Proverbs 31:10-11

Prayer Prompts:

- To encourage your husband's heart
- To be kind and transparent as you seek to fully trust one another

Day 16

Show Your Support

People are drawn to one another for a variety of reasons. Sometimes it is because they have similar interests. Those like passions can easily fuel a relationship. And yet some couples find that they actually have very little in common which can make that whole "thriving in marriage" thing a bit more difficult. Whether or not you and your husband are impassioned by the same things in life today I'd like to challenge you to show your support for him in an area that he is passionate about.

My husband and I both enjoy exercising. When we have the opportunity to get a work out in together it actually feels like a mini date night! It's easy for me to understand why he is drawn to this area of interest and vice versa. Pushing your body to the limit and seeing results is very rewarding. However, there are other areas of interest that we don't share... and may even struggle to fully understand. This scenario can easily transition into a "you do your thing and I'll do mine" mentality- which has some selfish motives if we're honest. What if instead of looking at these differences as "whatever floats your boat" we made an effort to come along side of each other and show our support?

Asking questions, showing an interest, and trying to better understand your spouse's hobbies and pursuits may help shine some light on why he enjoys them so much. This simple gesture of going out of your way to show that you care can speak volumes as to the amount of love you hold for him. It's a win-win!

And while we're on the topic of our "differences" I'd like to touch on something else for a moment. You know those quirky differences that you once found so attractive in your spouse... The ones that overtime eventually became frustrating to you? Have you ever thought of how those very differences, the ones that you struggle to understand and often hope to change, can actually be a blessing in disguise? It took me a while to realize this one, but a few years ago it finally hit me that I should be filled with gratitude that my husband is not just like me.

My perfectionist, organized, peaceful nature always imagined how much cleaner the house and calmer the atmosphere would be if my husband was also an organized neat freak who thrived on quietness and cleanliness. And then one day it hit me! What was I thinking?! If my husband was just like me then that would mean that he also would have extremely high expectations of me in these specific areas which is already stressful when trying to take care of two very active, energetic, and strong willed children.

I finally realized that the expectations I set for myself were more than enough.

Just because our strengths and weaknesses differ doesn't mean that one of us is in the wrong. When I step back and look at it, our differences truly do complement one another. We balance each other out much more than I ever realized- in a much needed and healthy way.

Please try to view your differences in this way. Not every difference is a blessing, and some may still be difficult to live with. If this is the case I challenge you to pray that God will work in your own heart instead of seeking to change your spouse.

"Let each of you look not only to his own interests, but also to the interests of others." Philippians 2:4

Prayer Prompts:

- To not have a condescending attitude toward your husband in regards to his interests in life
- For a desire to come along side of him to show your support and know how to go about doing so

Day 17

Make Him Breakfast

There's a reason they say the way to a man's heart is through his stomach. I don't think I've ever met a man who doesn't genuinely enjoy food! Start your morning off by making your husband a nice home cooked meal. Whether you whip up some bacon and eggs before he leaves for work or have the time to go all out and make an extravagant meal with all the fixings to serve him breakfast in bed please just make sure that you pour some love and effort into it. Serving in this small way can put a smile on his face and give him the confidence to tackle the day.

The idea of having a servant's heart within marriage is woven throughout this book, but I believe it's important to define what exactly is meant by this to clear up any confusion. *Serving* does not equal allowing ourselves to become a doormat. Although God desires for us to have humility I don't believe this mindset honors Him. God's Word makes it clear that as people made in His image we are to value one another.

By serving one another I'm referring to the idea of *giving of ourselves for the good of someone else.*

Have you ever thought about how God created our hearts to do this very thing? A simple act of service does not go unnoticed by our Maker. When we learn to take our eyes off of ourselves in order to help those around us we can't help but discover joy in the process.

Do you remember when Jesus washed his disciples feet? (John 13:1-17) He chose to humbly serve them in this way to demonstrate the importance of placing others before ourselves. Yes, God absolutely desires for us to be filled with joy, but contrary to popular belief, pleasing ourselves isn't the way to go about it. We are here to bring glory to our Creator and lovingly serve those He has placed in our lives which can bring about great joy for everyone involved. If our heart is so fixed on making ourselves happy above all else we will no doubt miss out on this sweet blessing.

"For you were called to freedom, brothers. Only do not use your freedom as an opportunity for the flesh, but through love serve one another. For the whole law is fulfilled in one word: "You shall love your neighbor as yourself." Galatians 5:13-14

Prayer Prompts:

- To have a true understanding of Biblical service and a desire to love your neighbor as yourself

Day 18

Play "Your Song"

When was the last time that you listened to "your song"? You know the first one that you slow danced to on your wedding day... The one that held meaning for both of you and made you think of one another every time you heard it? When was the last time that you actually danced together to it?

Tonight when the house is quiet, play your song and ask your husband to dance with you. You can light some candles to set the mood or if you're feeling extra ambitious string some white lights outside on your deck and dance under the stars.

There is a powerful connection in music and memory. Hearing a particular song that once upon a time held such meaning is likely to evoke some sweet memories and emotions that possibly haven't surfaced in a while. The goal here is not to get yourself all emotional, but to simply *remember*. To remember what initially drew you to your husband.

To remember how he made you smile... and how you delighted to go out of your way to make him smile in return. To remember why you chose him. *And why he chose you.*

You may feel like two very different people than you were on the day you said "I do", but remember that love is an action, not a feeling. If you chose to love him then, you can choose to love him now. One thing that I've learned in my own marriage is that emotions are never meant to be led with. Yes, they can certainly be healthy, but they can also steer us down a wrong path when we put them in the driver's seat.

When we're struggling with negative emotions toward our spouse I think it is best to hit pause and ask God for wisdom and clarity of thought in the situation. I memorized a helpful verse regarding our emotions many years ago that has served me well in times of struggle. Jeremiah 17:9 says "The heart is deceitful above all things, and desperately sick; who can understand it?" Simply put: our hearts can't always be trusted and can easily lead us astray.

Whether in marriage or otherwise, filter your struggles through God's Word and prayer, not the guidance of a fickle heart.

"If any of you lacks wisdom, let him ask God, who gives generously to all without reproach, and it will be given him." James 1:5

Prayer Prompts:

- For a desire to connect with your husband like you did in the beginning
- To cautiously guard your heart from negativity and discontentment

Day 19

Forgive Him

Today's challenge may be one of the most difficult. It is simple in theory, but can be incredibly hard to put into action: If you are struggling with some sort of bitterness in your heart towards your husband, forgive him. If he has hurt you or let you down in some way, *seek God's help to forgive him.*

As broken people living in a fallen world we will make mistakes and will be hurt by those we love. There is not a single marriage that is immune to the results of sin. Please remember that we have an enemy who desperately wants us to fail in this relationship and throw in the towel when the going gets tough. He will do everything in his power to drive a wedge between us and fill our hearts with pain, deception, and despair.

In our finite minds we struggle to see past the here and now, but the reality is that there is often a spiritual battle (Ephesians 6:12) taking place behind the scenes that can so easily destroy a marriage.

If you are in a difficult season of marriage (or even in the midst of a difficult few days) I encourage you to seek comfort in the arms of your Savior. There is no pain that you're experiencing that He hasn't felt (Hebrews 4:15). Scripture tells us that "God is near to the brokenhearted and saves the crushed in spirit" (Psalm 34:18). If you are hurting, God is hurting with you and He alone can be the One to fully mend your hurting heart. Seek Him for healing and then ask Him for strength to forgive the one who has hurt you so deeply.

Carrying the weight of bitterness around is a heavy burden to bear.

In my own marriage there have been times when the hurt runs deep for a significant reason. The crushing blow that numbs you for days isn't something that can be taken lightly. However, there have also been times when I've allowed my imagination to run wild and get myself all worked up over something rather insignificant. As women we just so happen to excel on making emotionally charged rash decisions in response to pain. I have learned that when we are hurt by the decisions of our spouse, we shouldn't automatically assume we know the entire story. Or even their intentions for making that decision in the first place.

When you feel as if your husband has wronged you pray for a humble heart to approach him with and simply ask if you've understood the situation correctly. Then gently explain to him why you were hurt and seek to restore your relationship. I'm not saying that this is an easy fix.

Hurt feelings don't just disappear. At times it may even be appropriate to seek the guidance of a professional for counseling. But when your love for your spouse is greater than your grudge, you will desire to make things right.

I'd like to take this one step further and also encourage you to seek that restoration sooner rather than later. I'll be honest and say that my husband is much further along in this one than I am! I truly admire him for his desire to restore our relationship so quickly when we've had a disagreement. I, on the other hand, have unfortunately been known to give the silent treatment at times until I'm fully ready to forgive.

This "waiting" does more harm than good. Scripture encourages us to forgive quickly for good reason. The longer we neglect to forgive someone the more room we allow for bitterness to creep in and lodge into our hearts.

"Be angry and do not sin; do not let the sun go down on your anger, and give no opportunity to the devil." Ephesians 4:26-27

Prayer Prompts:

- To seek God's strength and find comfort in Him when you've been deeply hurt
- To admit that you mess up and hurt your spouse too and to humbly seek his forgiveness
- For the wisdom to navigate trying situations in a way that honors God

Day 20

A Meaningful Photo

A picture is worth a thousand words- especially when it is a photo of you and the man you love. Today dig into your photos to find one of your favorite meaningful pictures of you and your husband. If you don't have a physical copy be sure to print one off. Once you've made your decision write a sweet note on the back explaining why this picture is so special to you. Then place it somewhere your husband is sure to find.

So what exactly is it that makes a photo meaningful? The location, lighting, landscape, or likes on social media? Obviously these are shallow answers that do not add value to a photo. *A photo is meaningful because of the cherished memories it represents.*

Let's be intentional in capturing more of those memories. Not just with our camera, but truly lock them away in our hearts. In a day and age of social media we can be so determined to snap the perfect picture that we neglect to soak up the moments that make up that picture.

As convenient as our cell phones are I'd like to challenge you to leave your phone at home more often in order to treasure time spent with your loved ones like you used to. And when you do capture the perfect snapshot try savoring the moment on your own rather than feeling the need to share it with the world.

When I think back to my own favorite family photos, the majority weren't taken at an elaborate event or special occasion. They were taken in a moment of silliness as we were making each other laugh. They were taken to remember a kind gesture or sweet moment. They were taken during something very routine and included nothing out of the ordinary. And yet these memories are the ones that are most precious to me.

What is something that you can do to ensure that you are creating more of these moments and memories with your spouse? We assume we have all the time in the world to make memories with those we love, but the reality is that time is fleeting.

May we lay aside the distractions. Slow down. And stop taking one another for granted.

"...you do not know what tomorrow will bring. What is your life? For you are a mist that appears for a little time and then vanishes." James 4:14

Prayer Prompts:

- To be more present and lay aside the distractions
- To realize the shortness of life and stop taking one another for granted

Day 21

Brag On Him

Our encouraging words can build up the heart of our husband more than we often realize. Speaking those words of approval, appreciation, and affirmation in front of others may just be the cherry on top! Today (or any day this week that would be appropriate) compliment or brag on your husband in front of someone else. Express your gratitude for and pride in your spouse *not only to him but also in the presence of others*. Complimenting him in this way can bring a little bit of joy into his heart as he rests in knowing that you are pleased with him.

If he was your handyman and fixed your furnace in the dead of winter saving you a boatload of money and time while restoring warmth to your family thank him for it! Then tell someone else how proud you are of him for figuring that out! If he has an admirable work ethic and just received a promotion, brag on him! Even if he didn't get that promotion, but works hard to provide for your family, express your gratitude for his dedication and efforts!

Is he coaching your little guy's basketball team even though basketball isn't really his sport? Thank him and brag on him for his desire to love on and lead those boys.

The things that initially impressed us in the beginning are often the very things that we take for granted down the road. Once we begin to peel back the expectancy of what has become ordinary to us we can see clearly enough to start to appreciate things like we used to.

All of a sudden the ordinary transforms into tiny bits of *extraordinary*. Please take a moment to think upon the extraordinary in your husband. What sets him apart? What was it that drew you to him all those years ago? Now take a moment to thank God for him. He is a gift.

"Every good gift and every perfect gift is from above, coming down from the Father of lights with whom there is no variation or shadow due to change." James 1:17

Prayer Prompts:

- To be grateful for your husband's strengths instead of dwelling on everything you'd like to change
- To know how to best encourage his heart

Day 22

A Favorite Restaurant

I don't know about you, but date nights are few and far between in our household. Life gets busy and before we know it it's been another three months since we last spent some quality one on one time together outside of the house. Today you get to surprise your husband by taking him out to his favorite restaurant just because. Turn a mundane weekday into a spontaneous night out just because you can.

I have learned the value of reconnecting in this way time and time again. Have you ever been guilty of convincing yourself that you're doing just fine because you're living under the same roof and communicating in a civil manor? Is the reality more like you're feeling miles apart and struggling? I've certainly been there. Planning intentional time out and about together not only has a way of providing each of us a breather, but it also gives us the ability to rekindle that spark as we set aside all of life's distractions to solely focus on each other and our marriage.

I once heard that marriage is like a garden. If we are faithful to put in the hard work of "tending and keeping" it... in time it will likely flourish.

On a side note, you may even opt to bring the kiddos along with you and make it a fun family night out every once and while! Although spending that one on one time together is vital to maintaining a healthy marriage, I believe that spending time together as a *family* also plays an important role in strengthening a marriage. We can become so busy with obligations and extracurricular activities that we spend very little time investing into the lives of our children. If you have children still at home I strongly encourage you to be intentional in creating lots of family time.

Bonding, laughing, playing, and learning together as a family unit can also draw a husband and wife closer to each other. I'll never grow tired of watching my husband pour into our children. It bolsters my affections for him every single time.

Play a family game together. Go on a walk or bike ride. Have a family movie night. Go on a hiking adventure. Pouring into our kids together as parents has a way of filling up our love tank too.

"Behold, children are a heritage from the Lord, the fruit of the womb a reward. Like arrows in the hand of a warrior are the children of one's youth. Blessed is the man who fills his quiver with them!" Psalm 127:3-5

Prayer Prompts:

- To be more intentional in the time you spend together as a family

Day 23

Let Him Lead

It wasn't until recent years that the idea of a husband leading his family became frowned upon, as if this somehow diminishes the worth of the wife. We seem to forget that our differences complement one another. They do not make us inferior to our husband in any way. Today, I'd like to encourage you to be more mindful of your words and actions when it comes to making decisions for your family. Let your husband fulfill his God given role and allow him to lead.

Have you ever taken the time to think upon the beauty of God's design for marriage? Even before sin ever entered the picture God purposefully created Eve specifically to satisfy the longings of Adam's heart when the rest of creation fell short. Her unique qualities perfectly complemented his and she became his suitable helper. His best friend. His encourager. His life partner. His love. His wife. The two became one flesh.

Can you even imagine the innocence, purity, and absolute perfection of love they must have shared?

A love untainted by sin and crafted by the very hand of God.

It's interesting to note that God didn't create a helper for Adam that had the exact same qualities that he did. No, this special helper was similar to him, but also very different. Whereas Adam was naturally strong, Eve was tender. Whereas men tend to be more competitive and assertive, women are more empathetic and nurturing. Men are driven by logic. Women thrive in the emotional arena. If we take a step back to look at the big picture we'll realize that embracing those differences is exactly what makes us fit together like a puzzle. Our differences create harmony in a marriage. They make a unified front even stronger.

I recently came across a quote that I believe is worth sharing. "A woman wants to be a man's equal, but an equal of a very special kind. At a deep and fundamental level she has a strong desire to be led, protected, and cared for." [1]
And at a deep and fundamental level our men want to lead! It is a blessing for them to be able to love on, provide for, guide, and protect their families. Just as it is a blessing for us as wives and mothers to be able to uplift, care for, and comfort our loved ones.

This certainly doesn't mean that we shouldn't have a say in situations. A man that truly loves his wife will desire her input because he values her. But it does mean that maybe we should keep our negative or opinionated thoughts to ourselves more often, trust in his judgement, and rest in the fact that his leadership ability frees us up from added responsibilities.

A man that leads his family well is a beautiful sight to see.

Whether your husband thrives in this area or is just getting his footing please be faithful to encourage and pray for him.

"For the husband is the head of the wife as Christ is the head of the church, his body, of which he is the Savior." Ephesians 5:23

Prayer Prompts:

- For your husband to find his confidence in Christ as he seeks to honor Him by leading his family well.
- For the wisdom and strength to know when to speak up and when to remain quiet

Day 24

Embrace Him

Have you ever wondered how a simple hug has the ability to calm a weary heart, soothe away anxious thoughts, or bring about joy? It's because of a happy little hormone called oxytocin that is released inside of our brains upon affectionate touch. We were made to embrace one another. Today, when the opportunity arises walk up to your husband and embrace him. Just hold him for a moment- no words necessary.

Hand holding, cuddling, and hugging all trigger the release of this incredible hormone which can lower stress levels and even build up the immune system! Meaningful touch between a husband and wife can strengthen a marriage. Yet it's often one of the first things we let slide when the pressures around us increase.

It's possible that your husband's primary love language is "physical touch" which means he genuinely needs a healthy dose of affection to feel loved. I'm not strictly referring to intimacy, but any form of positive physical contact.

My husband is affectionate by nature and inherited a strong desire to show love in this way within our marriage. These seemingly small gestures have made a profound impact on our relationship. The warmth of his actions express a depth of love that I didn't even know was possible.

The way a person communicates love is very often the way that they most desire to receive it. Discovering this about my own husband revealed his needs to me in a fresh way. I realize that not everyone is as comfortable showing affection, but I encourage you to make it more of a priority in your marriage. Reach for his hand or gently hold his arm when you're walking together. Snuggle up close to him on the couch. Curl up beside him to be his "little spoon" when you go to bed. Offer him a hug when he leaves for work *and when he returns home.*

Just for fun one day I decided to count how many times one of us reached out for a hug. Seven. And that was on a weekday, it's typically double on a weekend when we have more access to each other. Oxytocin seems to be doing its job for us and I imagine that it can for you and your husband too!

In marriage it is so often the smallest investments that can make the biggest return.

"His left hand is under my head, and his right hand embraces me!" Song of Solomon 2:6

Prayer Prompts:

- For a desire to be more affectionate with your husband
- To try to better understand and speak his love language

Day 25

Kid Free Evening

There are no words to express the amount of love and gratitude I hold in my heart for my children. There are also no words to express the amount of shock and surprise my husband and I experienced upon entering into parenthood. A very sweet but colicky baby girl wasn't exactly what I had envisioned as we drove home as a family of three for the first time.

This journey was unlike anything we'd ever imagined or fully prepared for. Stepping into these beautiful joy-filled roles as Mommy and Daddy was an adjustment period for us both. Understandably so, our time and attention became greatly divided. Our priorities changed, our schedules changed, our perspectives changed...just about everything changed. The one-on-one time my husband and I were used to sharing together was greatly diminished- for good reason of course, but it was still an adjustment period none the less. Our children have brought incredible joy into our lives and I cannot imagine life any different.

I've learned, however, that as little ones enter the picture we have to be all the more intent on protecting our marriage.

As a mom it can be unbelievably easy to allow our children to take priority over our spouse. We can even allow them to become idols in our life if we aren't careful. Yes, we absolutely must lovingly pour into our children, but not at the expense of our husband. Finding balance and prioritizing family is a must for keeping a marriage healthy.

Today, please do your best to find a sitter for your children so you can enjoy a kid free evening together (if that's not possible take the kids out for a few hours to allow your husband time to relax). You don't even have to leave the house. Sometimes it's nice to just take a breather at home in the peace and quiet without being needed. Let your husband decide what to do with his unexpected free evening and be content with his decision. Then take a moment to thank God for the quiet, thank Him for your husband, and thank Him for the incredible gift of children.

"Now they were bringing even infants to him that he might touch them. And when the disciples saw it, they rebuked them. But Jesus called them to him, saying, "Let the children come to me, and do not hinder them, for to such belongs the kingdom of God. Truly, I say to you, whoever does not receive the kingdom of God like a child shall not enter it."" Luke 18:15-17

Prayer Prompts:

- To faithfully invest in your marriage and know how to prioritize your husband and children

- To seek God for strength and wisdom as the parenting trials arise and work together as a team in tackling the difficulties

Day 26

Grateful For His Provision

I think it's safe to say that men have an innate desire to provide for their family. This God given desire to protect, lead, and provide is deeply wired within them. Please take some time today to express your gratitude for your husband's provision. Thank him for the way that he works hard to take care of your family.

Both the husband and the wife have unique roles when it comes to running a household and leading a family, but we can be certain that a husband and father finds immense satisfaction in knowing that he is faithfully providing. It may even be that the wife brings in a greater income, but provision encompasses more than just money. Does your husband provide security and stability? Does he plan, have a clear vision, and set goals for your family? Does he physically and emotionally protect? Does he meet the needs of you and your children? Then he is doing his job and providing in some capacity. Be grateful for the good and make sure he knows.

There may be other areas that you feel he is lacking in, but instead of nagging or harboring bitterness I'd encourage you to keep on showing gratitude. Genuine appreciation may just propel his heart into action in other areas as well.

"Give thanks in all circumstances; for this is the will of God in Christ Jesus for you." 1 Thessalonians 5:18

Prayer Prompts:

- To be grateful for the blessings that surround us instead of dwelling on unfulfilled desires in marriage and life.
- To thank God for His gracious provision

Day 27

Make Him Laugh

The further along we get in marriage the more we have a tendency to lose the light-heartedness and playfulness that was once such an integral part of our relationship. Although it is true that some of us are naturally more serious than others it doesn't mean that we should ever stop having fun and enjoying each other's company.

Today, look for a way to make your husband laugh. Bring up a funny memory. Flirt with him. Playfully poke fun at him. Go buy some water or nerf guns and have at it! Make him smile and have fun!

My husband and I have so many memories of us just laughing together. Anyone who knows him would easily describe him as a pretty funny guy (or a goofball might be a more appropriate word). He makes me smile and laugh so easily. And although I'm not naturally as quick-witted, I just so happen to be quite the dork and am able to make him laugh too. Laughter truly does the heart good and has been a welcome comfort in our marriage.

Apart from the obvious benefit of uplifting our spirits, laughter can also strengthen the bond of a husband and wife, deepen trust, relieve stress, ease tension, and even serve as a coping mechanism when dealing with grief. There is a reason that Scripture makes a point to say that a cheerful heart is good medicine (Proverbs 17:22).

Please don't get so wrapped up in your daily responsibilities that you forget how to laugh. Make an effort to bring about some laughter in your marriage. I promise you that it will do you both a whole lot of good!

"A joyful heart is good medicine." Proverbs 17:22a

Prayer Prompts:

- To appreciate the genuine joy of laughter and seek opportunities to bring about the smiles of others
- To not allow the stressors of life to overwhelm you and learn what it means to rest in Jesus

Day 28

Take A Walk

Most of us are aware of the multiple health benefits of walking. However we may not always consider the *non-physical* benefits, such as how walking with your spouse is an opportunity to foster a healthy emotional bond. Today ask your husband if he would like to join you for a walk. Be sure to share some of your favorite memories along the way.

Walking together as a couple is an easy way to prioritize intentional time spent together without the need to plan anything in advance. It's a simple way to reduce stress, get in some exercise, enjoy God's creation, and bond with the man you love.

My husband and I have been walking together since we adopted our sweet pup, Sam, more than ten years ago. After hundreds of walks we still never tire of unwinding together in this way. We have the added benefit of having our children along for the stroll nowadays too! They happily chat and bike on ahead of us while we hang back and enjoy each other's company.

I may slip my hand in his. He may offer me his arm. We might flirt a little, smile at each other, or just enjoy the walk in silence as we take in the beauty of creation and blessing of our sweet kiddos bicycling up ahead. There is something so calming about getting outside to enjoy God's creation. We have had some of the best laughs and giggles, seen some of the most beautiful sunsets, and made many precious memories on our walks.

I can honestly say that so often the best 30 minutes of my day happens when we're all together sharing our thoughts, holding hands, giving (and getting) piggyback rides, meeting new animals along the way and saying hello to passersby. Even after some occasional trip ups and meltdowns I very rarely return home from a walk in a sour mood. There is something special about a walk outdoors that does wonders for the soul.

I encourage you to make family walks a tradition if you are able to. A leisurely stroll together can strengthen your bond, encourage your heart, and help you to better appreciate the little things in life.

"The heavens declare the glory of God, and the sky above proclaims his handiwork." Psalm 19:1

Prayer Prompts:

- For the clarity to see the many blessings that surround you
- To take care of the health you've been given
- To discover new ways of bonding with your husband

Day 29

Candlelight Dinner

Do you realize that God is the Author of romance? The sweet excitement and mystery we experience in a loving marriage relationship was instituted by the Creator of the universe, not by Hollywood. And it is actually a beautiful depiction of the kind of love He holds for us.

I'd like to encourage you to add a little romance into your evening tonight. Take some time planning and preparing a nice home cooked meal for your husband, and enjoy it together by candlelight. You may have to wait until after the kiddos go to bed (or have your older children enjoy a picnic style dinner in another room for a set time). It may not be entirely convenient, but please make an effort to make it count. Set aside the electronics and distractions, make the house quiet, and just enjoy each other's company. Share, ask questions, and build up the heart of your husband. (Your efforts may even set the mood for some more of that initiating we talked about on day 8!)

Although romance can be an indicator of a healthy marriage, it cannot be the *foundation* of a marriage.

Our culture has a tendency to depict love as a happily ever after fairytale romance. Deep down we know that we are imperfect people and this idea is unrealistic, but we fall for it anyway- *hook, line, and sinker...* And become sorely disappointed along the way as we discover that our Prince Charming actually has failures and flaws.

A marriage built on the ideal of effortless happiness is one destined to fail from the beginning. To the contrary, we must faithfully pour into our marriage, on the easy days and challenging days alike. Marriage takes commitment, patience, gratitude, endurance, trust, teamwork, humility, forgiveness and grace, among other things. At times it may even require *sacrifice* as we learn what it means to genuinely place our spouse's needs above our own.

The biblical definition of love beautifully describes God's intention for the marriage relationship. "Love is patient and kind; love does not envy or boast; it is not arrogant or rude. It does not insist on its own way; it is not irritable or resentful; it does not rejoice at wrongdoing, but rejoices with the truth. Love bears all things, believes all things, hopes all things, endures all things." (1 Corinthians 13:4-7)

Love "bearing" and "enduring" all things is a far cry from the culture's encouragement to "follow our hearts". When we make the decision to endure the difficulties in marriage rather than walk away, we open the door for growth. Those very trials are what allow us to stretch and grow in our character, marriage, and faith.

May we be faithful to pursue God's ideals for our marriage rather than the ideals of the world around us.

And may we offer our husband grace as we remember that there is no such thing as perfection this side of Heaven.

Going back to those fairy tale love stories... I can't help but think that there's a reason that we're so drawn to them.
The desire for this kind of love, chivalry, kindness, purity, and romance seem to be ingrained in the depths of every female's heart. Perhaps because our Creator made us this way. *Perhaps to even point us to the perfect and unconditional love of the One who died to be our Savior.*

"Let us rejoice and exult and give him the glory, for the marriage of the Lamb has come, and his Bride has made herself ready..." Revelation 19:7

Prayer Prompts:

- To recognize the deception of our culture's ideals for marriage, and not be led astray by them
- To understand the depth of Jesus' love for you in a fresh way

Day 30

Bake His Favorite Dessert

There's something special about a homemade dessert that was crafted with one specific person in mind. Last night you spent a good amount of time creating a romantic dinner for two. Tonight you get to top it off by preparing your husband's favorite dessert to enjoy together as a family after dinner. Once you've got his favorite in mind spend a little bit of time searching for a top notch version and go for it! If you're not the greatest baker, please don't fret, just know that your kind gesture and efforts will make his dessert all the more sweet.

I remember growing up how my mom would cook a favorite dinner and bake a favorite dessert every year for our birthday. The extra effort she put into making our special day that much more special truly brought joy to my heart, as I know it did hers too. Please put some love into your creation and give it your best. Remember that when we begin to go out of our way *to give of ourselves for the good of someone else* there's something transformative that takes place in our heart too.

Do it for no other reason than because you want to be a blessing to your husband and I'm certain that you'll reap some blessings as well.

You may even want to consider surprising him with a small meaningful gift during dessert. Your husband's primary love language could possibly be *receiving gifts*. This doesn't mean that he is materialistic or shallow by any means, but that the act of giving elicits a more heartfelt response in him. Being on the receiving end of someone else's kindness makes quite an impact on these men. Although receiving a gift any time of the year is such a thoughtful gesture, I will say that in my own experience, those surprise out-of-the-blue gifts have typically been the most cherished. To know that someone saw something that reminded them of you or noticed a small detail about you and went on a mission to find the perfect gift makes you feel loved, indeed.

"Put on then, as God's chosen ones, holy and beloved, compassionate hearts, kindness, humility, meekness, and patience, bearing with one another and, if one has a complaint against another, forgiving each other; as the Lord has forgiven you, so you also must forgive. And above all these put on love, which binds everything together in perfect harmony." Colossians 3:12-14

Prayer Prompts:

- For a desire to love on and serve others for no other reason than to be a blessing to them
- To take notice of the little details about your spouse in an effort to make him feel noticed and loved

Day 31

Look Him In The Eyes

When I initially began digging a little deeper studying the Bible I was blown away at the depth of meaning behind the original Hebrew and Greek words. Unfortunately the English language cannot fully convey the meaning of every biblical text, which means that, occasionally, we lose some important details in translation.

There are four types of love mentioned in the Bible that are all translated into our single English equivalent:

- *Eros-* Romantic love
- *Storge-* The affection of family members, such as in a parent/child relationship
- *Philia-* Brotherly love and respect for others
- *Agape-* Sacrificial and unconditional

A healthy marriage consists of two of these forms of love-*eros* and *agape*. The romantic love we hold for one another in marriage is part of what sets this unique bond apart from all the rest.

Our Creator's beautiful design in bringing a man and wife together to become one flesh is parallel to none in terms of human relationships. As special as this type of love is it pales in comparison to the kind of love our Savior holds for us- *agape.* Yet, this Christ-like, self-sacrificing, unconditional love is exactly what we are called to in marriage. It is only when we approach marriage with this kind of love at the core that it will truly begin to thrive.

The servant's heart mentality that flows freely throughout these pages is nothing more than agape love in action.

Today, when the timing is right and you have his full attention look your husband in the eyes and say "I love you". These three little words hold a lot of weight. Make sure your attitude towards him is fueled by a genuine sacrificial love.

"Therefore be imitators of God, as beloved children. And walk in love, as Christ loved us and gave himself up for us, a fragrant offering and sacrifice to God." Ephesians 5:1-2

Prayer Prompts:

- To understand the true meaning of sacrificial love
- For the strength to love and forgive your spouse when he has wronged you

Thank you for your dedication and commitment to pour into your spouse during this challenge. My prayer is that it has helped you better appreciate the gift of marriage and the gift of your husband.

Please remember that although there is tremendous beauty in the marriage design a perfect marriage simply doesn't exist. As part of a fallen creation each and every one of us marry a sinner. There will be moments that we struggle to treat our spouse as we should. There will be moments when we don't feel loved and have little desire to show love in return. During these trials please remember that our love for our spouse is a reflection of our love for God. By choosing to love him during his not so lovable moments (and vice versa) we're able to catch a tiny glimpse of the love our Savior holds of us.

When two people look at marriage as an opportunity to love and serve one another, it is truly beautiful indeed.

Let's build up our husbands and go love them well.

A Love Untainted

The human heart longs to be loved. And if we're honest, we don't just want any kind of love, deep down our longing is for a perfect love. One that won't leave us bruised and broken. One that finds value in us and will accept us without conditions. One that offers forgiveness and grace when we are most underserving. We long for a love that will never fail us nor forsake us.

It is a love that can never be attained- outside of the finished work of Jesus. God crafted our hearts in such a way that we can catch tiny glimpses of this love, along with beauty, joy, comfort, and peace in the world that surrounds us because He is the Author of each of these, but those glimpses will always be momentary. They will forever fade away until we seek ultimate fulfillment in the One who died to be our Savior.

Our spouse, children, loved ones, and friends will let us down. There is only one love that is untainted by sin- the love of Christ. If you have faithfully read these pages there is a good chance that you would already consider yourself to be a believer. But I'd like to ask you to please take a moment to examine your own heart.

We are living in a world that encourages us to follow and trust our hearts because deep down we're all "pretty good" people. However, God's Word (which acts like a mirror to show us the true picture) tells us the very opposite. Our hearts are deceitful. They are wicked and deep down we are actually sinful people in desperate need of redemption. We have all allowed anger to overtake us, lied, lusted, stolen, and coveted to some degree among other things (Exodus 20). When we compare our reality with God's pure and holy standard we realize just how far we fall short (Romans 3:23). But it doesn't end there...

If we take a step back to look at the Bible as a whole we will see that it is a love story. A beautifully woven together love story from the very first pages of Genesis to the end of Revelation. It is the true story of a God whose love for the people He created is beyond comprehension. His plan all along was to dwell among us, but that plan was marred when we gave into sin. The crazy thing is that He didn't just turn His back on us as a result of our rebellion. Far from it! He gently convicts and pursues us longing for the moment we realize our need for Him. Not because He needs us, but that in spite of our sinful hearts He actually wants us!

He desires for us to realize that we were created with a void that was only ever meant to be filled by Him.

And then... God sent His perfect sinless Son, Jesus, to earth for the sole purpose of dying the death that we deserve in order to offer us a sweet gift of grace. If we genuinely repent of our sin, believe and accept what Christ did for us on the cross, and that He rose again three days later to prove His defeat over death, then we can be assured of an eternity spent with Him in Heaven.

The original Greek meaning of the word "repent" means "to change one's mind or purpose". Repentance isn't simply feeling sorry for what we've done or even simply asking forgiveness for it (although both of these are a natural response to it). Repentance is a change in our hearts over our sin as we realize the hurt we have caused our Maker, and are completely broken as a result.

Repentance is the result of a heart that has been transformed by the perfect love it has been searching for all along.

Yes, my prayer is that your marriage will be strengthened in some small way as a result of reading this book. But my ultimate desire is that your heart will be transformed as you fully grasp the unconditional love of Jesus.

Seek Him, Friend, and you will find Him. (Jeremiah 29:13)

48 Conversation Starters

Please don't ever stop asking questions and getting to know your spouse. Here is a list of conversation starters if you're looking for some topics of discussion. Get comfortable, cozy up, and ask away! (If you would like a free printable card version of this list please feel free to visit: https://ajoyfueledjourney.com/48-conversation-starters-for-married-couples/)

1. What is a favorite family tradition you had growing up?
2. What is one of your craziest dreams?
3. What is one of your most impressionable childhood memories?
4. At what point did you first realize that you were in love with your spouse?
5. What is one of your favorite memories of your time dating?
6. How would you describe your perfect day?
7. If you could legally own any animal as a pet what would it be?
8. When was the last time you laughed until you cried?
9. What was a favorite hobby of yours growing up that you don't do anymore?

10. If you could only eat one food for the rest of your life what would it be?
11. What do you find most attractive about your spouse?
12. What do you think your spouse's primary love language is?
13. What do you love most about your spouse's personality?
14. What is something that you miss from your childhood?
15. If you had 24 hours to do anything at all what would you do?
16. If you could travel anywhere in the world, but had to stay there for a year where would you go?
17. What is an area that your spouse could be of encouragement/ help keep you accountable in?
18. What is something you would like to begin doing together as a couple?
19. What is one way that I can better meet your needs?
20. Who currently holds the greatest amount of influence over you?
21. On the day you die what will be most important to you?
22. What is the most enjoyable part of being married?
23. What's the funniest thing that happened to you this week?
24. When was the last time you had a pillow fight?
25. If you could have any talent what would you choose?
26. Nerf gun or water gun fight?
27. If you were given the ability to change one thing about the world what would it be?
28. What was your greatest accomplishment over the last year?
29. What do you love most about your family?

30. What is your favorite thing to do together as a couple?
31. What is your favorite memory from your wedding day?
32. What is a good way to make your spouse smile?
33. What is your all-time favorite movie?
34. Name 3 odd/little known facts about yourself
35. Would you rather go forever without ice cream or pizza?
36. If you could recreate any date that you've gone on which one would you choose?
37. If you could relive an entire month of your marriage when would you choose?
38. What is your ideal amount of physical intimacy each month?
39. What do you most need from your spouse?
40. What do you like best about being a husband/wife?
41. Would you rather receive a love letter or homemade sweet treat?
42. What was going through your mind the moment you first met your spouse?
43. What is a quirky trait that you find attractive about your spouse?
44. What is one of your favorite outfits that your spouse wears?
45. If you could rewrite your wedding vows for this very moment what would you say?
46. If you could go back and change anything about your life what would you choose?
47. What is one thing you admire about your parents?
48. What is one thing you hope to instill within your children?

52 Date Ideas

Outdoor

- Stargazing
- Trip to the zoo/ Aquarium
- Picnic
- Hiking
- Arboretum/ Conservatory
- Drive-In Theater
- Miniature Golf
- Go Karting
- Batting Cages/ Driving Range
- Kayak
- Tennis
- Park Trails
- Fruit Farm
- Fishing
- Farmers Market
- Camping
- Zip-lining
- Sporting Event
- Amusement Park
- Taco Truck Tour
- Hot Air Balloon Ride
- Paintball Soft
- Trail Ride

Indoor

- Rock Climbing
- Gym
- Concert
- Play/ Theater/ Musical
- Marriage Retreat

- Ice Cream Parlor/ Bakery
- Ballroom Dancing Lessons
- Cooking Class
- Museum
- Painting Class
- Escape Room
- Dog Shelter (to play with the dogs)
- Coffee Shop
- Ice Skating
- Mystery Dinner Theater
- Orchestra
- Glow-in-the-dark Miniature Golf
- Serve at a soup kitchen
- Bowling
- Board Game Café
- Axe Throwing

At Home

- Bike ride
- Nerf/water gun/snowball fight
- DIY project
- Pillow fight
- S'mores and conversation cards
- Game/ movie night
- Candlelight dinner
- Puzzle

Notes

Day 3

1. Chapman, Gary. *The Five Love Languages.* Chicago, Northfield Publishing, Reprint edition (January 1, 2015)

Day 12

1. Bible Hub. HELPS Word-Studies 1618. Ektenés. Accessed January 1, 2022 through https://biblehub.com/greek/1618.htm

Day 23

1. Focus On The Family (2015). Key Differences Between Male and Female. Accessed January 6, 2022 through https://www.focusonthefamily.com/family-qa/key-differences-between-male-and-female/

In Closing

Writing on the topic of marriage was a bit out of my comfort zone. I certainly never imagined writing a whole book on the subject. I am far from an expert in this area and honestly feel unqualified and inadequate to share much of anything resembling marriage advice. However, a few short months into my blogging journey (which primarily focuses on parenting since that is where the majority of mine and my husband's struggles lie) I wrote a little post entitled "Build Him Up" that opened my eyes to the struggles younger generations, like mine, are facing in regards to marriage. Even though the bulk of my content is in the motherhood and parenting niche, for some reason that specific post from a couple of years ago continues to bring in more traffic than almost any other.

In spite of the trials of raising two incredibly sweet but iron-willed children (one of whom also has multiple special needs) God graciously continues to bless our marriage. Our marriage is not perfect by any means, but we have learned some tidbits over the years that I believed were worth sharing.

I don't have all the answers and still have a long way to go on this journey, but thankfully I do know that One who instituted marriage and am grateful for the many words of wisdom He has provided us in His Word. This book was a simple attempt to nudge us back in line with God's original intent for creating "one flesh".

It didn't seem right to write about a month long commitment if I wasn't willing to do it myself. So in an effort to be completely transparent with you I thought I would share my own experience going through this challenge in such a busy and trying phase of life. For starters it took me six weeks to complete. Some days I was so excited to surprise my husband and put every ounce of effort into it. Other days I completely forgot that I was even supposed to be doing a challenge! There were days when I attempted to catch up and check two off my list and I although I tried I didn't always do them in the right order. I say all of that to let you know that I didn't "nail it", and yet I still found myself genuinely enjoying pouring into my husband and becoming all the more grateful for him.

What I didn't expect was how my appreciation for my Savior also grew. Writing about this topic and putting it all into action had a way of revealing to me the love He holds for me on an even deeper level. It is a humbling thought to know that the God of the universe continues to gently pursue us and love us entirely in spite of our brokenness, rebellion, and sin. If you do not yet know Him, please seek Him before it is too late. He will never fail you.

Thank you again for taking the time over these last few weeks to deny yourself some comforts and conveniences in an effort to give of yourself for the good of your spouse!

Hearing from my readers truly does my heart good! If you would like to share any thoughts, comments, or questions after reading this book please feel free to reach out to me at tabatha@ajoyfueledjourney.com or visit the site at AJoyFueledJourney.com.

♡ *Tabatha*